Section Goals

Letter Basics

Learn the cursive alphabet.

B B B

Word Formation

Combine letters to form words.

Confident

Fluidity

Convert print to cursive.
Develop fluid handwriting.

Simple is sexy.

Personality

Add style, flair, & individuality.

A A A A A

a a a a a a a a a a

a a a a a a a a a a

a a a a a a a a a a

a

a

a a a a a

a a a a a

a a a a a

a

a

$\mathcal{B}$ $\mathcal{B}$ $\mathcal{B}$ $\mathcal{B}$

$\mathcal{B}$ $\mathcal{B}$ $\mathcal{B}$ $\mathcal{B}$

$\mathcal{B}$ $\mathcal{B}$ $\mathcal{B}$ $\mathcal{B}$

$\mathcal{B}$

$\mathcal{B}$

b b b b b

b b b b b

b b b b b

b

b

$\mathcal{C}$ $\mathcal{C}$ $\mathcal{C}$ $\mathcal{C}$ $\mathcal{C}$

$\mathcal{C}$ $\mathcal{C}$ $\mathcal{C}$ $\mathcal{C}$ $\mathcal{C}$

$\mathcal{C}$ $\mathcal{C}$ $\mathcal{C}$ $\mathcal{C}$ $\mathcal{C}$

$\mathcal{C}$

$\mathcal{C}$

c c c c c

c c c c c

c c c c c

c

c

D D D D

D D D D

D D D D

D

D

d d d d d

d d d d d

d d d d d

d

d

Ɛ Ɛ Ɛ Ɛ Ɛ

Ɛ Ɛ Ɛ Ɛ Ɛ

Ɛ Ɛ Ɛ Ɛ Ɛ

Ɛ

Ɛ

e e e e e e

e e e e e e

e e e e e e

e

e

$\mathcal{F}$ $\mathcal{F}$ $\mathcal{F}$ $\mathcal{F}$

f f f f

H H H H H

H H H H H

H H H H H

H

H

h h h h h

h h h h h

h h h h h

h

h

$\mathcal{L}$ $\mathcal{L}$ $\mathcal{l}$ $\mathcal{l}$ $\mathcal{l}$

$\mathcal{l}$ $\mathcal{l}$ $\mathcal{l}$ $\mathcal{l}$ $\mathcal{l}$

$\mathcal{l}$ $\mathcal{l}$ $\mathcal{l}$ $\mathcal{l}$ $\mathcal{l}$

$\mathcal{l}$

$\mathcal{l}$

i i i i i i i

i i i i i i i

i i i i i i i

i

i

𝒥 𝒥 𝒥

𝒿 𝒿 𝒿 𝒿

K K K K

K K K K

K K K K

K

K

k k k k k

k k k k k

k k k k k

k

k

$\mathscr{L}$ $\mathscr{L}$ $\mathscr{L}$ $\mathscr{L}$

$\mathscr{L}$ $\mathscr{L}$ $\mathscr{L}$ $\mathscr{L}$

$\mathscr{L}$ $\mathscr{L}$ $\mathscr{L}$ $\mathscr{L}$

$\mathscr{L}$ $\mathscr{L}$ $\mathscr{L}$ $\mathscr{L}$

$\mathscr{L}$

l l l l l l l

l l l l l l

l l l l l l

l

l

$\mathcal{m}$ $\mathcal{m}$ $\mathcal{m}$

m m m

$\mathcal{N}$ $\mathcal{N}$ $\mathcal{N}$ $\mathcal{N}$

$\mathcal{N}$ $\mathcal{N}$ $\mathcal{N}$ $\mathcal{N}$

$\mathcal{N}$ $\mathcal{N}$ $\mathcal{N}$ $\mathcal{N}$

$\mathcal{N}$

$\mathcal{N}$

n n n n

n n n n

n n n n

n

n

O O O O

O O O O

O O O O

O

O

O O O O O O

O O O O O O

O O O O O O

O

O

$\mathcal{P}$ $\mathcal{P}$ $\mathcal{P}$ $\mathcal{P}$ $\mathcal{P}$

$\mathcal{P}$ $\mathcal{P}$ $\mathcal{P}$ $\mathcal{P}$ $\mathcal{P}$

$\mathcal{P}$ $\mathcal{P}$ $\mathcal{P}$ $\mathcal{P}$ $\mathcal{P}$

$\mathcal{P}$

$\mathcal{P}$

p p p p p

p p p p p

p p p p p

p

p

$\mathcal{Q}$ $\mathcal{Q}$ $\mathcal{Q}$ $\mathcal{Q}$ $\mathcal{Q}$

$\mathcal{Q}$ $\mathcal{Q}$ $\mathcal{Q}$ $\mathcal{Q}$ $\mathcal{Q}$

$\mathcal{Q}$ $\mathcal{Q}$ $\mathcal{Q}$ $\mathcal{Q}$ $\mathcal{Q}$

$\mathcal{Q}$

$\mathcal{Q}$

q q q q q q

q q q q q q

q q q q q q

q

q

R R R R

R R R R

R R R R

R

R

r r r r r r

r r r r r r

r r r r r r

r

r

S S S S

S S S S

S S S S

S

S

s s s s s s

s s s s s s

s s s s s s

s

s

$\mathcal{T}\ \mathcal{T}\ \mathcal{T}\ \mathcal{T}$

$\mathcal{T}\ \mathcal{T}\ \mathcal{T}\ \mathcal{T}$

$\mathcal{T}\ \mathcal{T}\ \mathcal{T}\ \mathcal{T}$

$\mathcal{T}$

$\mathcal{T}$

$t\ t\ t\ t\ t\ t$

$t\ t\ t\ t\ t\ t$

$t\ t\ t\ t\ t\ t$

t

t

𝒰 𝒰 𝒰 𝒰

𝒰 𝒰 𝒰 𝒰

𝒰 𝒰 𝒰 𝒰

𝒰

𝒰

𝓊 𝓊 𝓊 𝓊 𝓊

𝓊 𝓊 𝓊 𝓊 𝓊

𝓊 𝓊 𝓊 𝓊 𝓊

𝓊

𝓊

$\mathcal{V}$ $\mathcal{V}$ $\mathcal{V}$ $\mathcal{V}$ $\mathcal{V}$ $\mathcal{V}$

$\mathcal{V}$ $\mathcal{V}$ $\mathcal{V}$ $\mathcal{V}$ $\mathcal{V}$ $\mathcal{V}$

$\mathcal{V}$ $\mathcal{V}$ $\mathcal{V}$ $\mathcal{V}$ $\mathcal{V}$ $\mathcal{V}$

$\mathcal{V}$

$\mathcal{V}$

v v v v v

v v v v v

v v v v v

v

v

W W W

W W W

W W W

W

W

w w w w

w w w w

w w w w

w

w

𝒳 𝒳

𝓍 𝓍

Y Y Y Y

Y Y Y Y

Y Y Y Y

Y

Y

y y y y y

y y y y y

y y y y y

y

y

Letter Review

A a

B b

C c

D d

E e

F f

G g

H h

I i

J   *j*

K   *k*

L   *l*

M   *m*

N   *n*

O   *o*

P   *p*

Q   *q*

R   *r*

S   *s*

Memorization

Study the letters you have practiced, then turn the page. Try to write them without a cursive example to replicate.

Don't worry if you can't remember how to write them all. Do your best. This book provides four chances to memorize all the letters, so make a copy of the pages if you want additional memorization attempts.

Memorization #1

Write each upper and lower-case letter in cursive. Can't remember how one is written? Skip it and continue with the others. Once you're done, you can look at the previous section for help.

(Don't worry if this section difficult. You'll have more chances to memorize the cursive alphabet. Do your best. You'll get better each time you practice.)

A   a

B   b

C   c

D   d

E   e

F   f

G   g

H   h

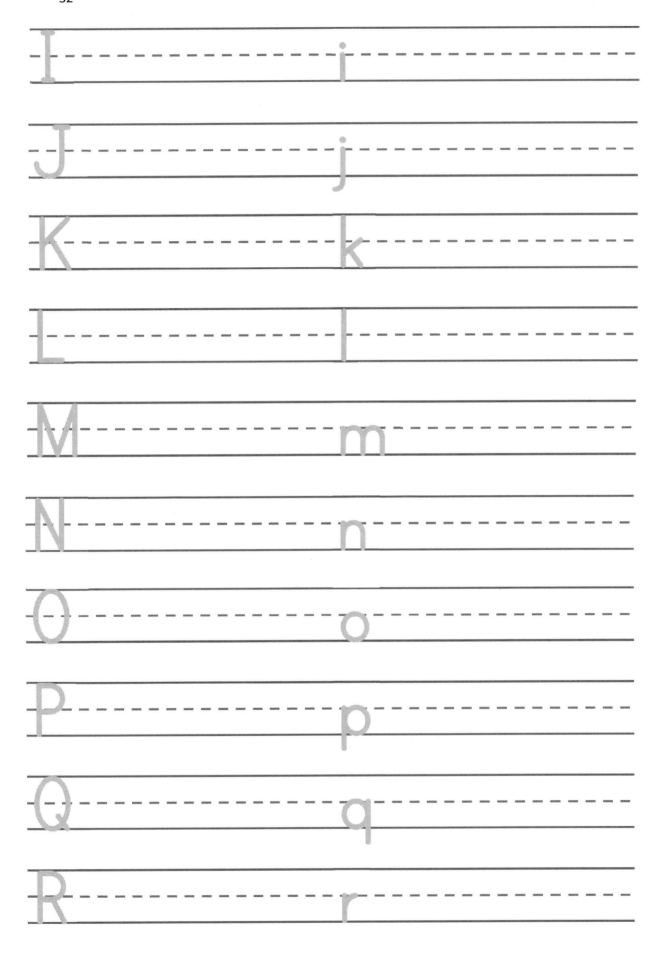

S   s

T   t

U   u

V   v

W   w

X   x

Y   y

Z   z

How did you do? Check the box next to the letters you got right. Leave the letters you couldn't remember blank. This way you can see how much you've learned the next time you practice.

A□ a□   B□ b□   C □ c □   D□ d□   E □ e□

F □ f□   G□ g□   H □ h □   I □ i □   J□ j□

K□ k□   L□ l □   M□ m□   N□ n□   O□ o□

P□ p□   Q□ q□   R □ r □   S□ s□   T□ t□

U□ u□   V□ v□   W□ w□   X□ x□   Y□ y□

Z□ z□

Memorization #2

Can you do better than last time?

Write each upper and lower-case letter in cursive. If you can't remember how one is written, skip it and continue with the others. Look up the ones you don't know when you're finished.

A — — — — — — — — — — — — a — — — — — — — — — — — — —

B — — — — — — — — — — — — b — — — — — — — — — — — — —

C — — — — — — — — — — — — c — — — — — — — — — — — — —

D — — — — — — — — — — — — d — — — — — — — — — — — — —

E — — — — — — — — — — — — e — — — — — — — — — — — — —

F — — — — — — — — — — — — f — — — — — — — — — — — — —

G — — — — — — — — — — — — g — — — — — — — — — — — — —

H — — — — — — — — — — — — h — — — — — — — — — — — — —

I   i

J   j

K   k

L   l

M   m

N   n

O   o

P   p

Q   q

R   r

S ----------------------- s -----------------------

T ----------------------- t -----------------------

U ----------------------- u -----------------------

V ----------------------- v -----------------------

W ----------------------- w -----------------------

X ----------------------- x -----------------------

Y ----------------------- y -----------------------

Z ----------------------- z -----------------------

How did you do? Check the box next to the letters you got right. Leave the letters you couldn't remember blank. This way you can see how much you've learned the next time you practice.

A□ a□   B□ b□   C□ c□   D□ d□   E□ e□
F□ f□   G□ g□   H□ h□   I□ i□   J□ j□
K□ k□   L□ l□   M□ m□   N□ n□   O□ o□
P□ p□   Q□ q□   R□ r□   S□ s□   T□ t□
U□ u□   V□ v□   W□ w□   X□ x□   Y□ y□
Z□ z□

Memorization #3

Try to get them all this time. You can do it.

Write each upper and lower-case letter in cursive. If you can't remember how one is written, skip it and continue with the others. Look up the ones you don't know when you're finished.

A ——————————————— g

B ——————————————— b

C ——————————————— c

D ——————————————— d

E ——————————————— e

F ——————————————— f

G ——————————————— g

H ——————————————— h

I i

J j

K k

L l

M m

N n

O o

P p

Q q

R r

S   s

T   t

U   u

V   v

W   w

X   x

Y   y

Z   z

How did you do? Check the box next to the letters you got right. Leave the letters you couldn't remember blank. This way you can see how much you've learned the next time you practice.

A□ a□   B□ b□   C □ c □   D□ d□   E□ e□
F□ f□   G□ g□   H □ h □   I □ i □   J□ j□
K□ k□   L□ l□   M□ m□   N□ n□   O□ o□
P□ p□   Q□ q□   R□ r □   S□ s□   T□ t□
U□ u□   V□ v□   W□ w□   X□ x□   Y□ y□
Z□ z□

Memorization #4

This is the last memorization lesson.

Copy these pages if you would like additional attempts to memorize the letters.

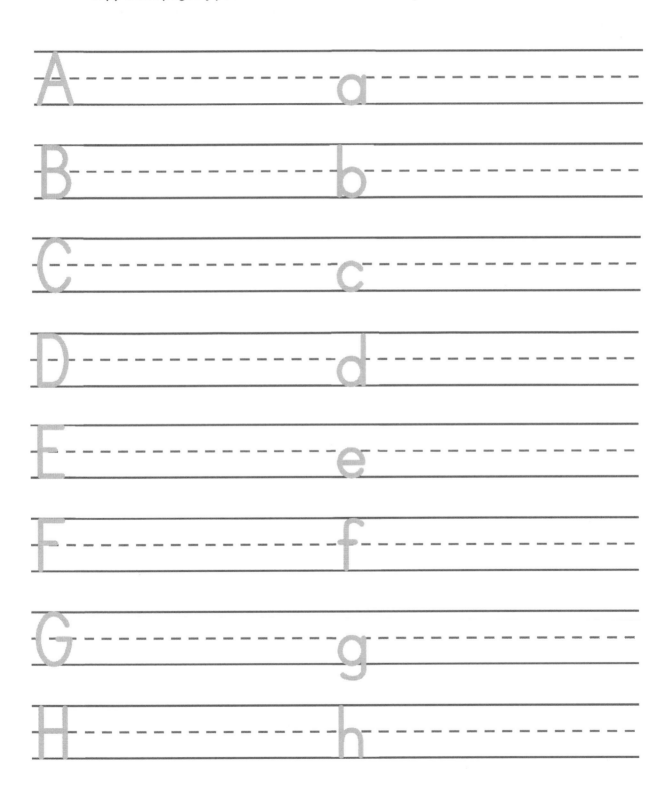

I   i

J   j

K   k

L   l

M   m

N   n

O   o

P   p

Q   q

R   r

S   s

T   t

U   u

V   v

W   w

X   x

Y   y

Z   z

How did you do? Check the box next to the letters you got right. Leave the letters you couldn't remember blank. This way you can see how much you've learned the next time you practice.

A□ a□   B□ b□   C□ c□   D□ d□   E□ e□
F□ f□   G□ g□   H□ h□   I□ i□   J□ j□
K□ k□   L□ l□   M□ m□   N□ n□   O□ o□
P□ p□   Q□ q□   R□ r□   S□ s□   T□ t□
U□ u□   V□ v□   W□ w□   X□ x□   Y□ y□
Z□ z□

Word Formation

Learn to combine cursive letters by tracing, then copying the words provided.

Pay attention to how the letters connect with each other.
Write these words without lifting your pencil or pen.

Alluring authenticity

Brave Bold bodacious

Cozy Confident creative

Dreamy Daring desire

Enchanting eloquence

Fearless Faithful friend

Gentle Glowing grace

Hot Happy handsome

Irresistible imagination

Just Joyfully jazzy

Kind Kinetic kissable

Loving Loyal lusty

Modestly mesmerizing

Naturally noteworthy

Openly opportunistic

Purpose Passion patient

Quick Quirky quaint

Relaxed radiance

Sweet Sexy sassy

Tough Timeless truth

Uniquely uplifting

Vibrantly voluptuous

Warm Willed wonder

Xenial Foxy exuberant

Yummy yearning

Zen Zestful zazzle

Extra Practice

Were any of the words or letters more challenging to write than the others?
Use the remaining lines to practice them now.

Converting Words

In this section words will be given to you in standard format. You need to convert them to cursive and write them on the lines provided. Notice that you've written these words already. Try to write them in cursive without looking back for help. Be brave. Test your memory. Once you're done you can check your answers with the words in the previous section.

Alluring authenticity

Brave Bold bodacious

Cozy Confident creative

Dreamy Daring desire

Enchanting eloquence

Fearless Faithful friend

Gentle Glowing grace

Hot Happy handsome

Irresistible imagination

Just Joyfully jazzy

Kind Kinetic kissable

Loving Loyal lusty

Modestly mesmerizing

Naturally noteworthy

Openly opportunistic

Purpose Passion patient

Quick Quirky quaint

Relaxed radiance

Sweet Sexy sassy

Tough Timeless truth

Uniquely uplifting

Vibrantly voluptuous

Warm Willed wonder

Xenial Foxy exuberant

Yummy yearning

Zen Zestful zazzle

Extra Practice

Were any of the words or letters more challenging to write than the others?
Use the remaining lines to practice them now.

Answers

These are the answers for this section

Alluring authenticity

Brave Bold bodacious

Cozy Confident creative

Dreamy Daring desire

Enchanting eloquence

Fearless Faithful friend

Gentle Glowing grace

Hot Happy handsome

Irresistible imagination

Just Joyfully jazzy

Kind Kinetic kissable

Loving Loyal lusty

Modestly mesmerizing

Naturally noteworthy

Openly opportunistic

Purpose Passion patient

Quick Quirky quaint

Relaxed radiance

Sweet Sexy sassy

Tough Timeless truth

Uniquely uplifting

Vibrantly voluptuous

Warm Willed wonder

Xenial Foxy exuberant

Yummy yearning

Zen Zestful zazzle

Converting Mixed Words

Here are new words to practice writing in cursive.

Need help or want to check your work? Answers are shown on the top of page 58.

Resilient Focused

Charismatic Honest

Inquisitive Perceptive

Nonchalant Flexible

Brazen Perseverance

Candid Honorable

Sensual Compassion

Generous Reliable

Intelligent Versatile

Spontaneous Playful

Optimistic Proactive

Humorous Easygoing

Curious Motivational

Answers

Answers for this section can be found on the next page.

Answers

These are the answers for the previous section

Resilient Focused
Charismatic Honest
Inquisitive Perceptive
Nonchalant Flexible

Brazen Perseverance
Candid Honorable
Sensual Compassion
Generous Reliable
Intelligent Versatile

Spontaneous Playful
Optimistic Proactive
Humorous Easygoing
Curious Motivational

Converting Sentences

Convert the following text into cursive sentences.
(Turn the page to check your answers.)

Form these dazzling

words carefully. Write

them now. Chillax later."

"Turn your face to the

_____

- - - - - - - - - - - - - - - - - - -

_____

sun and your shadows

_____

- - - - - - - - - - - - - - - - - - -

_____

will fall behind you."
~New Zealander Proverb

- - - - - - - - - - - - - - - - - - -

_____

"If you can't live longer,

_____

- - - - - - - - - - - - - - - - - - -

_____

live deeper."
~Italian Proverb

*Turn the page to
check your answers.*

_____

- - - - - - - - - - - - - - - - - - -

_____

Write a few more lines

then get a coffee and

some chocolate.

Your mind and hand

deserve a rest.

"Dignity does not

consist in possessing

honors, but in

deserving them."

~Aristotle

Answers

Page 58: *"Form these dazzling words carefully. Write them now. Chillax later."*
Page 59: *"Turn your face to the sun and your shadows will fall behind you."*
"If you can't live longer, live deeper."

"Shared joy is a double

joy; shared sorrow is

half a sorrow."
~ Swedish Proverb

"The heart that loves

is always young."
~Greek Proverb

"It does not matter

how slowly you go

as long as you

do not stop."
~Confucius

Answers

Page 60: *"Write a few more lines then get a coffee and some chocolate. Your mind and hand deserve a rest."*

Page 61: *"Dignity does not consist in possessing honors, but in deserving them."*

Your confidence and

skills are growing.

Allow the words to flow.

Let the curves dance

from your fingertips.

"The reputation of a

thousand years may be

determined by the

conduct of one hour."
~Japanese Proverb

Answers

Page 62: "Shared joy is a double joy; shared sorrow is half a sorrow."
"The heart that loves is always young."

Page 63: "It does not matter how slowly you go as long as you do not stop."

"When you are content

to be simply yourself

and don't compare

or compete, everybody

will respect you."
~Lao Tzu

"Difficulties strengthen

the mind as labor

does the body."
~Seneca the Younger

"Once bitten, twice shy."
~Australian Proverb

Answers

Page 64: *"Your confidence and skills are growing. Allow the words to flow. Let the curves dance from your fingertips."*

Page 65: *"The reputation of a thousand years may be determined by the conduct of one hour."*

"Better a little which

is well done, than a

great deal imperfectly."
~Plato

"The very essence of

romance is uncertainty."
~Oscar Wilde

Writing on Single Lines

Dashed lines are great for learning to write letters, but eventually it's important to learn to form letters without the aid of these extra lines. Now is your chance to practice. Create each letter carefully and try to write them using the same shape and size as you had before.

"When the going

gets tough, the

tough get going."

~English Proverb

Answers

Page 66: *"When you are content to be simply yourself and don't compare or compete, everybody will respect you."*

Page 67: *"Difficulties strengthen the mind as labor does the body."*
"Once bitten, twice shy."

Go on, time to be bold.

Give your letters a little

sass. You've worked

hard for these curves.

Show them off.

"Our greatest glory is

not in never failing,

but in rising every

time we fail."

~Confucius

Answers

Page 68: *"Better a little which is well done, than a great deal imperfectly."*
"The very essence of romance is uncertainty."

Page 69: *"When the going gets tough, the tough get going."*

"Do not say a little

in many words but a

great deal in a few."
~Pythagoras

"Believe you can and

you're halfway there."
~Theodore Roosevelt

"Wealth consists not

in having great

possessions, but in

having few wants."
~Epictetus

Answers

Page 70: *"Go on, time to be bold. Give your letters a little sass.*
You've worked hard for these curves. Show them off."
Page 71: *"Our greatest glory is not in never failing, but in rising every time we fail."*

"We are like chameleons,

we take our hue and

the color of our moral

character, from those

who are around us."
~John Locke

"In the end, it's not

_____

the years in your life

_____

that count. It's the

_____

life in your years."

~Abraham Lincoln

_____

Answers

Page 72: *"Do not say a little in many words but a great deal in a few."*
"Believe you can and you're halfway there."

Page 73: *"Wealth consists not in having great possessions, but in having few wants."*

"Words should be

---

weighed, not counted."
~Yiddish Proverb

"The only true wisdom

---

is in knowing you

---

know nothing,"
~Socrates

Your determination

is amazing. You can

learn and accomplish

anything you wish.

Answers

Page 74: *"We are like chameleons, we take our hue and color of our moral character, from those who are around us."*

Page 75: *"In the end, it's not the years in your life that count. It's the life in your years."*

"Be yourself; everyone

else is already taken."
~Oscar Wilde

"It's better to light a

candle than curse

the darkness."
~Chinese Proverb

"Never let the fear of

striking out keep you

from playing the game."
~Babe Ruth

"Measure twice, cut once."
~Many cultures have a variation of this proverb.

Answers

Page 76: "Words should be weighed, not counted."
"The only true wisdom is in knowing you know nothing."

Page 77: "Your determination is amazing.
You can learn and accomplish anything you wish."

"When I let go of

what I am, I become

what I might be."
~Lao Tzu

"Whoever gossips to you

will gossip about you."
~Spanish Proverb

"I'd rather die of passion

---

than of boredom."
~Vincent van Gogh

"A beautiful thing

---

is never perfect."
~Egyptian Proverb

Answers

Page 78: *"Be yourself; everyone else is already taken."*
"It's better to light a candle than curse the darkness."

Page 79: *"Never let the fear of striking out keep you from playing the game."*
"Measure twice, cut once."

Writing Smaller

Most of the time you will not have large areas to write on. When converting these sentences focus on forming your letters smaller. Do this carefully so that your writing remains elegant and uniform. The habits you establish now will be hard to break later. Make sure they're good habits.

Don't worry about what people think of you.

They'll be jealous of your handwriting either way.

"A closed mind is like a closed book;

just a block of wood."
~Chinese Proverb

"Always forgive your enemies;

nothing annoys them so much."
~Oscar Wild

"Time never gets tired of running."
~Egyptian Proverb

If only you had a penny for every word you've written.

"Happiness and freedom begin with one principle.

Some things are within your control and some are not."
~Epictetus

"Cowards die many times before their deaths;

the valiant never taste of death but once."
~William Shakespeare (Julius Caesar, Act 2, Scene 2)

"Well done is better than well said."
~Benjamin Franklin

"In the midst of chaos, there is also opportunity."
~Sun Tzu

"Make the best use of what's in your power

and take the rest as it happens."
~Epictetus

Answers

Page 80: "When I let go of what I am, I become what I might be."
"Whoever gossips to you will gossip about you."

Page 81: "I'd rather die of passion than of boredom."
"A beautiful thing is never perfect."

"We are what we repeatedly do.

Excellence then is not an act, but a habit."
~Aristotle

"Luck is not chance, it's toil;

Fortune's expensive smile is earned."
~Emily Dickinson

"It is not the strongest of the species that survives,

---

not the most intelligent that survives.

It is the one that is the most adaptable to change."
~Charles Darwin

"Two good talkers are not worth one good listener."
~Chinese proverb

"With enough courage, you can do without a reputation."
~Margaret Mitchell

"A ship is safe in harbor, but that's not what ships are for."
~John A. Shedd

"People wear sexy cloths to get attention and boost

their confidence. Sexy handwriting has the same power.

Take your time to practice these curves. Let your speed

build naturally. You're developing the handwriting that

will represent your thoughts and voice. Will your written

words be comparable to a ballroom gown or tuxedo,

or will they resemble a tattered pair of sweatpants?

Answers

Page 82: Don't worry about what people think of you.
They'll be jealous of your handwriting either way.
"A closed mind is like a closed book; just a block of wood."
"Always forgive your enemies; nothing annoys them so much."
"Time never gets tired of running."
"If only you had a penny for every word you've written."

Page 83: "Happiness and freedom begin with one principle.
Some things are within your control and some are not.."
"Cowards die many times before their deaths;
the valiant never taste of death but once."
"Well done is better than well said."
"In the midst of chaos, there is also opportunity."
"Make the best use of what's in your power and take the rest as it happens."

"Nature does not hurry, yet everything is accomplished."
~Lao Tzu

"He who asks is a fool for five minutes

---

but he who does not ask remains a fool forever."
~Chinese Proverb

"Our incomes are like our shoes;

---

if too small they gall and pinch us;

---

but if too large, they cause us to stumble and to trip."
~John Locke

"All you need in life is ignorance and confidence,

---

and then success is sure."
~Mark Twain

"When love is not madness, it is not love."
~Spanish Proverb

"By failing to prepare, you are preparing to fail."
~Benjamin Franklin

"Courage isn't having the strength to go on –

it is going on when you don't have the strength."
~Napoleon Bonaparte

"I know nothing in the world that has as much

power as a word. Sometimes I write one

and I look at it, until it begins to shine."
~Emily Dickinson

"I shall stick to my resolution of writing always

what I think no matter whom it offends."
~Julia Ward Howe

Answers

Page 84: "We are what we repeatedly do. Excellence then is not an act, but a habit."

"Luck is not chance, it's toil; Fortune's expensive smile is earned."

"It is not the strongest of the species that survives, not the most intelligent that survives. It is the one that is the most adaptable to change."

"Two good talkers are not worth one good listener."

"With enough courage, you can do without a reputation."

"A ship is safe in harbor, but that's not what ships are for."

Page 85: People wear sexy cloths to get attention and boost their confidence.. Sexy handwriting has the same power. Take your time to practice these curves. Let your speed build naturally. You're developing the handwriting that will represent your thoughts and voice. Will your written words be comparable to a ballroom gown or tuxedo, or will they resemble a tattered pair of sweatpants?

"Life is mostly froth and bubble,

Two things stand like stone.

Kindness in another's trouble,

Courage in your own."
~Adam Lindsay Gordon

"If I had my life to live over again, I would have

---

made a rule to read some poetry and listen

---

to some music at least once every week."
~Charles Darwin

"Tact is the art of making a point

---

without making an enemy."
~Isaac Newton

"Great acts are made up of small deeds."
~Lao Tzu

"The only person you are destined to become

is the person you decide to be."
~Ralph Waldo Emerson

"Of all sad words of tongue or pen,

the saddest of these, 'It might have been.'"
~John Greenleaf Whittier

"Believe nothing you hear, and only half that you see."
~Edgar Allen Poe

"Everything is sketchy. The world does nothing but sketch."
~Florence Nightingale

"An ant on the move does more than a dozing ox."
~Lao Tzu

Answers

Page 86: "Nature does not hurry, yet everything is accomplished."
"He who asks is a fool for five minutes, but he who does not ask remains a fool forever."
"Our incomes are like our shoes; if too small they gall and pinch us; .
but if too large, they cause us to stumble and to trip."
"All you need in life is ignorance and confidence, and then success is sure."
"When love is not madness, it is not love."
"By failing to prepare, you are preparing to fail."

Page 87: "Courage isn't having the strength to go on – it is going on when you don't have the strength."
"I know nothing in the world that has as much power as a word. Sometimes I write one
and look at it, until it begins to shine."
"I shall stick to my resolution of writing always what I think no matter whom it offends."

"The pen is mightier than the sword." Your words are

---

gaining beauty and power with every day of practice.

"Experience is the teacher of all things."
~Julius Caesar

History doesn't repeat itself, but it often rhymes."
~Mark Twain

"If you do not change direction

---

you may end up where you are going."
~Lao Tzu

"We live in an age when unnecessary things

---

are our only necessities."
~Oscar Wilde

"It is always legitimate to wish to rise above

---

one's self, never above others."
~Julia Ward Howe

"You can never do a kindness too soon,

for you never know how soon it will be too late."
~Ralph Waldo Emerson

"It is never too late to be what you might have been."
~George Eliot

"If you want to go fast, go alone.

If you want to go far, go together."
~African Proverb

"A spoon does not know the taste of soup,

nor a learned fool the taste of wisdom."
~Welsh Proverb

Answers

Page 88: "Life is mostly froth and bubble. Two things stand like stone.
Kindness in another's trouble, Courage in your own."
"If I had my life to live over again, I would have made a rule
to read some poetry and listen to some music at least once every week."
"Tact is the art of making a point without making an enemy."
"Great acts are made up of small deeds."

Page 89: "The only person you are destined to become is the person you decide to be."
"Of all sad words of tongue or pen, the saddest of these, 'it might have been.'"
"Believe nothing you hear, and only half of that you see."
"Everything is sketchy. The world does nothing but sketch."
"An ant on the move does more than a dozing ox."

I wish the voices in my head would shut up.

Don't they realize I'm trying to write here?

"The most difficult thing is the decision to act,

---

the rest is merely tenacity."
~Amelia Earhart

"Some cause happiness wherever they go;

---

others whenever they go."
~Oscar Wilde

"And, of course men know best about everything,

---

except what women know better."
~George Eliot

"Everyone is kneaded out of the same dough,

---

but not baked in the same oven."
~Yiddish Proverb

"Coffee and love taste best when hot."
~Ethiopian Proverb

"Cheese, wine, and friends get better as they age ."
~Cuban Proverb

"Tell me who your friends are,

so I can tell you who you are."
~Bulgarian proverb

"Just because you do not take an interest in politics

doesn't mean politics won't take an interest in you."
~Pericles

"Some people go through a forest and see no firewood."
~English Proverb

Answers

Page 90: "The pen is mightier than the sword." Your words are
gaining beauty and power with every day of practice.
"Experience is the teacher of all things."
"History doesn't repeat itself, but it often rhymes."
"If you do not change direction you may end up where you are going."
"We live in an age when unnecessary things are our only necessities."
"It is always legitimate to wish to rise above one's self, never above others."

Page 91: "You can never do a kindness too soon, for you never know how soon it will be too late."
"It is never too late to be what you might have been."
"If you want to go fast, go alone. If you want to go far, go together."
"A spoon does not know the taste of soup, nor a learned fool the taste of wisdom."

"Day by day, what you choose, what you think and

what you do is who you become."
~Heraclitus

"What you leave behind is not what is engraved in stone

monuments but what is woven into the lives of others."
~Pericles

"Anger is an acid that can do more harm to the vessel in

which it is stored than to anything on which it is poured."
~Seneca

"It's not what you look at that matters, it's what you see."
~Henry David Thoreau

"Art is never finished, only abandoned."
~Leonardo da Vinci

"We don't inherit the earth from our ancestors,

we borrow it from our children."
~Native American Proverb

You've made such progress. Never stop writing.

Your letters and words look wonderful, but it's the

thought and the feelings behind your words that

matter most. Your words are too important to be

locked away. Share them with others.

"Either write something worth reading

or do something worth writing."
~Benjamin Franklin

Answers

Page 92: I wish the voices in my head would shut up. Don't they realize I'm trying to write here?
"The most difficult thing is the decision to act, the rest is merely tenacity."
"Some cause happiness wherever they go; other whenever they go."
"And, of course men know best about everything, except what women know better."
"Everyone is kneaded out of the same dough, but not baked in the same oven."

Page 93: "Coffee and love taste best when hot."
"Cheese, wine, and friends get better as they age."
"Tell me who your friends are, so I can tell you who you are."
"Just because you do not take an interest in politics
doesn't mean politics won't take an interest in you."
"Some people go through a forest and see no firewood."

Personality

You've learned the basics. Now you're ready to break the rules and develop a writing style of your own. Try making your letters more or less slanted. Experiment with lower case "g" and "y" to make their loops longer, shorter, rounder, or narrower. *Find what looks good to you. Find what feels natural.*

You may have already adapted some letters in the previous sections. These changes were probably instinctive. Now it's time to be intentional about your penmanship.

It's time to craft your sexy handwriting.

Capital Letters

You've learned how to write capital cursive letters. In practice, many people combine elements of standard print and cursive to make capital letters. Hybrid capital letters if you will. Mastering some of these and using them at the start of your sentences can add a surprising amount of flair to your writing.

Selecting unique capital letters is also the easiest way to create a distinctive signature. It might be best to find the capital letters in your name and practice the different styles. Some might look intimidating, but most are not too difficult. Practice your favorites for a few minutes and you'll probably agree. The great part is, the more difficult they seem, the more impressive they'll look to others.

We've provided some common variations for each capital letter in future pages, but don't limit yourself to this book. Look online for more ideas. There are hundreds.

Answers

Page 94: "Day by day, what you choose, what you think and what you do is who you become."
"What you leave behind is not what is engraved in stone monuments
but what is woven into the lives of others."
"Anger is an acid that can do more harm to the vessel in
which it is stored than to anything on which it is poured.."
"It's not what you look at that matters, it's what you see."
"Art is never finished, only abandoned."
"We don't inherit the earth from our ancestors, we borrow it from our children."

Page 95: You've made such progress. Never stop writing. Your letters and words look wonderful,
but it's the thought and the feelings behind your words that matter most.
Your words are too important to be locked away. Share them with others.
"Either write something worth reading or do something worth writing."

Signature Basics

Your signature is powerful. It's used on legally binding documents to identify you. A signature is used countless times throughout a lifetime. It's worth crafting well. *It's worth being proud of.*

1. **<u>Keep It Simple</u>:** A unique signature is important, but don't get carried away. You want one that's simple enough to write quickly and consistently.

2. **<u>Be Consistent</u>:** If your signature looks different each time, it will be difficult to prove when it's yours (or when it isn't). That can cause big problems.

3. **<u>First and Last Name</u>:** Signing documents with a first and last name is best practice. It's not required in most countries or situations, but it's still advisable. You also want people to be able to read it and know it belongs to you.

4. **<u>Use Letters</u>:** In most countries, a signature doesn't need letters. You could draw a cat if you want. If you intend for it to represent you and are consistent in using it this way, it generally counts as a signature. Yet, most don't recommend a drawing alone. It's best to use your full name in conjunction with a drawing.

5. **<u>Cursive or Print</u>:** It seldom matters from a legal standpoint. You could print your signature if you want. Since you purchased this book it's safe to assume you prefer a cursive signature. Most people do. Cursive is perceived as being more elegant and sophisticated. Cursive is often more distinctive and difficult to forge.

6. **<u>Have a Goal</u>:** What is your purpose for crafting a great signature? Do you just want it to be easy and legible? Pick a style that accomplishes that. Do you want your signature to be flashy? Consider making the first letters larger, circle or underline your signature, or include a trailing line at the end. These are easy ways to make your signature stand out.

Knowing what you want from your signature will help you decide how to craft it. Ask yourself what you want your signature to represent. What do you want it to convey? Develop a goal for your signature and design it accordingly.

Crafting Your Signature

We'll use the name Lily to help illustrate this process.

1. Start with the capital letters:

- ○ Cursive or print?
- ○ Large or small?
- ○ Wide or narrow?
- ○ Fancy or plain?

2. Add noncapital letters:

- ○ Large or small?
- ○ Wide or narrow?
- ○ Fancy or plain?

3. Try adding lines:

- ○ Beginning lines or trailing lines?
- ○ Curved lines or straight lines?
- ○ Long lines or short lines?
- ○ Loops or angles?

4. Linking first and last names:

- ○ Can your names be linked together?
- ○ Do you want them linked together?

(Some letters are easier to link than others)

5. Search for more ideas:

There are many variables to consider when crafting a signature. They can't all be covered in this book. A lot will depend on the letters in your name.

Look for ideas and resources on the internet. Whole video channels are dedicated to creating unique signatures. Check them out. Test new styles. Combine styles until you find one you like.

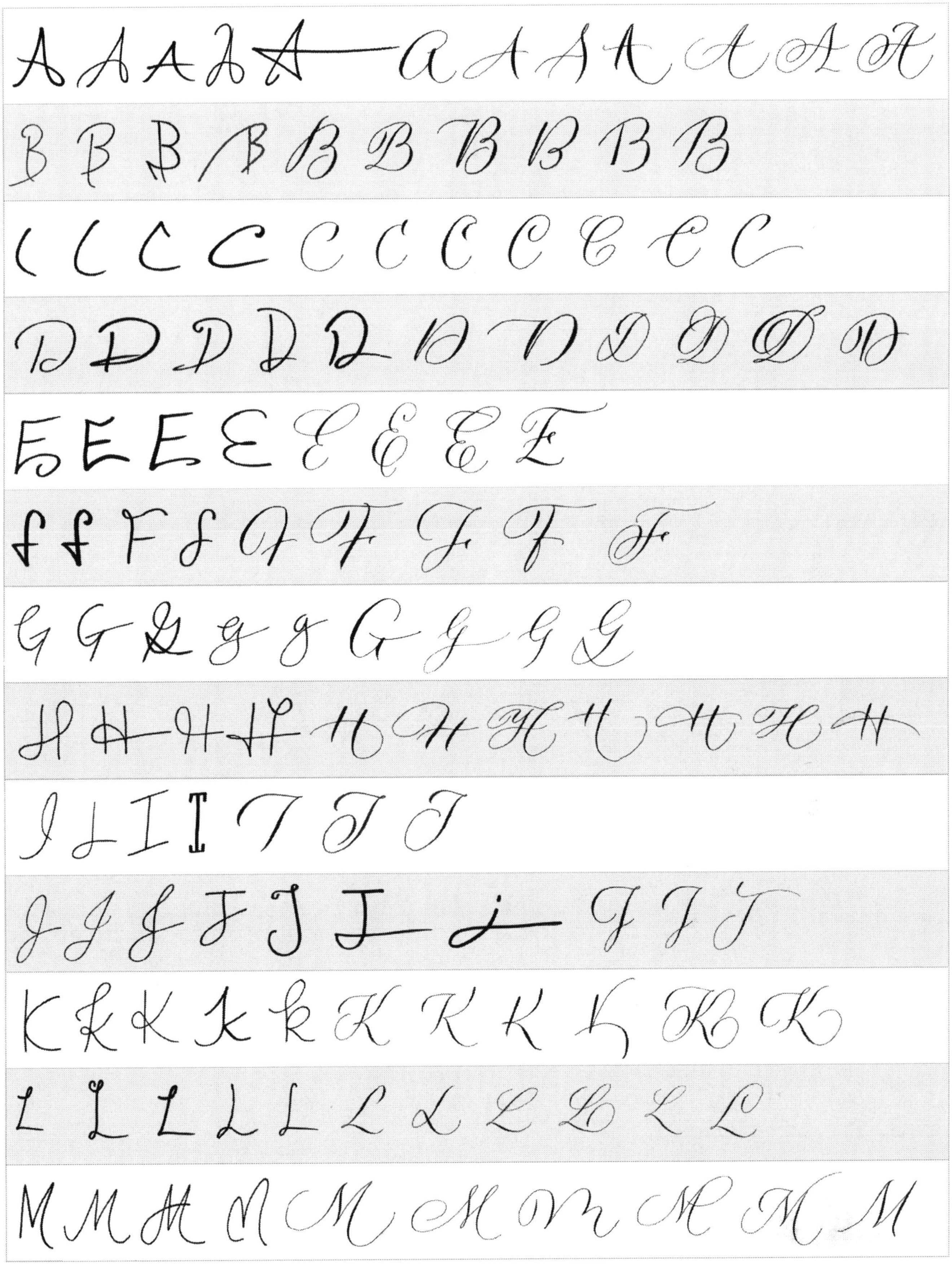

N N N N N N N

O O O O

P P P P P P P P P P P

Q Q Q Q Q Q Q Q Q Q Q

R R R R R R R R R R R

S S S S S S S S S S S

T T T T T T T T T T T

U U U U U U U U U U

V V V V V V V V V V V

W W W W W W W W W W W

X X X X X X X X X X X

Y Y Y Y Y Y Y Y Y Y Y

Z Z Z Z Z Z Z Z Z Z Z

Signature Practice

_____	_____
_____	_____
_____	_____
_____	_____
_____	_____
_____	_____
_____	_____
_____	_____
_____	_____
_____	_____
_____	_____
_____	_____

Signature Practice

_____   _____

_____   _____

_____   _____

_____   _____

_____   _____

_____   _____

_____   _____

_____   _____

_____   _____

_____   _____

_____   _____

Signature Practice

Signature Practice

Signature Practice

Signature Practice

Signature Practice

Signature Practice

_____   _____

_____   _____

_____   _____

_____   _____

_____   _____

_____   _____

_____   _____

_____   _____

ISBN: 978-1-63578-541-8

Current contact information for Libro Studio LLC can be found at www.LibroStudioLLC.com